Native Irish
DOGS

······························

Shane McCoy & Colin White

ABOUT THE AUTHORS

SHANE MCCOY

Shane McCoy holds a degree in Literature and Celtic Civilisation along with a Masters degree in Literature and Publishing from the National University of Ireland, Galway.

A publishing professional and keen dog enthusiast with a love of Irish history and an academic background in Celtic mythology, the author has lovingly collected and compiled information, factual and mythological, about the native Irish dog breeds.

COLIN WHITE

Colin White has been working in the publishing industry for six years on a wide variety of projects with large companies, as well as smaller organisations.

Travelling the length and breadth of the country, the avid photographer has captured images that convey the beautiful nature of Ireland's nine outstanding native dog breeds.

CONTENTS

FOREWORD

The dogs of Ireland are a reflection of its people. They reflect its history, lifestyle and mythology, and are an integral part of our culture and heritage. From the hounds that were exclusively the dogs of kings, to the gun dogs favoured by the earls, and the terriers of the farmers and peasants, all fulfilled a vital role over the centuries in our social history and development.

They are recognised worldwide for their beauty and working abilities, and for such a small nation we have brought some exceptional breeds to the world of dogs.

Over the years, the promotion and protection of these native breeds has been the responsibility of a few dedicated individuals, families, and, since its foundation in 1922, the members of the Irish Kennel Club. As some are in danger of extinction, the Irish Kennel Club has requested that the Department of Arts, Heritage and the Gaeltacht award them 'heritage status' in an effort to ensure their future. We hope we can achieve this next year.

I am personally delighted with this publication and I hope those who read it will gain a real understanding of the breeds that are part of the very DNA of being Irish.

Sean Delmar
President, Irish Kennel Club

Cú Faoil

IRISH WOLFHOUND

··

CALM, DIGNIFIED, COURAGEOUS

Cú Faoil
IRISH WOLFHOUND

BREED	LIFESPAN	KENNEL CLUB GROUP	VULNERABLE NATIVE BREED
Irish Wolfhound	6–9 years	Hound/FCI Group 10	No

UTILISATION
A sighthound, this breed was originally used as a dog of war and would pull men from horseback during battle. Later they were used for hunting wolves – from which the breed gets its name – wild boar and other large animals, as well as serving as a watchdog.

GENERAL APPEARANCE
The Irish Wolfhound is without doubt the most famous of the Irish breeds. Coming face-to-face with these gentle giants, their formidable size cannot be ignored, with males being a minimum height of 79cm at the shoulder and weighing at least 54.5kg. The Wolfhound should be longer than it is tall, and look fast enough to catch a wolf and strong enough to kill it. The overall frame of the Wolfhound should be similar in structure to that of a greyhound, or indeed any other sighthound. The coat is rough and hard to the touch, but is especially wiry and long over the eyes and under the jaw.

The breed comes in a variety of colours: grey, brindle, red, black, white, fawn and wheaten. They are graceful and muscular animals, built for speed, with extremely good vision.

PERSONALITY AND TEMPERAMENT
Despite its immense size, the Wolfhound is a placid, quiet dog, generally independent and reserved in character. The breed is summed up easily in its historic motto 'gentle when stroked, fierce when provoked'. Although independent, they thrive with human companionship and are loyal to their family. Again, contrary to their size, Wolfhounds are of a gentle and calm disposition, and are very tolerant of children. An easy dog to train, they respond well to calm and consistent leadership. However, these dogs are not good guard dogs and will tend to watch the family rather than defend territory or possessions.

Although the breed history suggests otherwise, the modern Wolfhound is a kind and patient companion that enjoys worldwide popularity. In owning a Wolfhound you can expect a loyal and devoted companion and wonderful guardian. Surprisingly for a dog this size, they do not require a huge amount of exercise, and a long walk to expend any energy will suffice – they will then happily laze around the house for the rest of the day.

BREED HISTORY

Once known as The Great Hound of Ireland, it is thought that the Wolfhound arrived with the Celts, who were present in Ireland around the 3rd century BC. These huge hounds, called *Cú Faoil*, were bred as hunting dogs and upon arriving on Irish shores they continued to be bred for the same purpose, while also taking up the job of protecting homes and livestock. One of the most ancient breeds, they were viewed as a status symbol and were only permitted to be owned by the kings and nobility of Ireland. The number of hounds each person was permitted to own was relative to his position within his kingdom. These great hounds were held in such high esteem that sometimes battles were fought over them.

We can learn a great deal about this ancient breed from Irish mythology and folklore. One of the most well-known stories is *The Legend of Cú Chulainn*. Setanta, also known as Cú Chulainn, was an ancient Gaelic warrior who was gifted with superhuman strength, speed and skill. At a young age Setanta left home to join the Red Branch Knights, and one day the blacksmith of King Conchobar, Culann, noticed his skill and invited him to a feast in his home. Unfortunately, Setanta was late arriving at the house and the feasting had already begun. Worse still, the hounds had been released. Suddenly, one of the hounds rushed forward to attack him and Setanta hurled his *sliotar* down the hound's throat, killing it. Hearing the commotion, the feasting party ran out to see what was happening. Setanta, although glad to be alive, was saddened at the sight of the dead hound, and offered to take the hound's place until Culann found a replacement. From that day forward, Setanta was called Cú Chulainn – the hound of Culann.

In the 16th, 17th, and early part of the 18th century, there was such a demand for the Irish Wolfhound throughout the royal houses of Europe and Scandinavia that it led to the near extinction of the breed in Ireland. In 1652, noting the decrease in the Irish Wolfhound population and a subsequent increase in the wolf population in Ireland, a declaration was signed banning the exportation of hounds from Ireland due to their scarcity. It is reported that the last wolf in Ireland was killed in county Carlow near Mount Leinster in 1786. After the eradication of wolves the Wolfhound once again suffered a sharp decline in numbers, mainly due to the fact its main prey animal was now extinct. The Irish Famine of the 1700s also played a factor in the breed's decline, as people were no longer able to feed such a large animal when there were no wolves left to hunt. As a result, Wolfhound numbers declined to such an extent that many thought the breed had been wiped out entirely. Thankfully, a few individuals kept the breed alive, and in later years it was through the work of Captain G. A. Graham that the breed was successfully revived, a feat achieved by sourcing pedigree Irish Wolfhounds and cross-breeding them with the closely related Scottish deerhounds.

From dwindling numbers and near extinction, the breed today is known internationally and enjoys huge popularity.

CARE

Extremely easy to care for, the Wolfhound's coat is essentially self-maintaining and a brush through every couple of weeks will suffice. Apart from a daily walk, they are easy dogs to care for. Due to their size, they will naturally eat far more than smaller breeds, and feeding one can be costly. Irish Wolfhounds would do best in a large house with a large garden or in a country setting.

DID YOU KNOW?

By the year AD 391, the Irish Wolfhound was known in Rome, when the first authentic mention of it was recorded by the Roman Consul, Quintus Aurelius, who had received seven of these magnificent dogs which 'all Rome viewed with wonder' as gifts.

Brocaire Buí

IRISH SOFT-COATED WHEATEN TERRIER

·······································

HAPPY, FRIENDLY, DEVOTED

Brocaire Buí
IRISH SOFT-COATED WHEATEN TERRIER

BREED	**LIFESPAN**	**KENNEL CLUB GROUP**	**VULNERABLE NATIVE BREED**
Irish Soft-Coated Wheaten Terrier	10–13 years	Hound/FCI Group 3	No

UTILISATION
Wheaten Terriers were originally bred as an all-purpose farm dog. Wheatens had a range of uses on the farm, which included hunting vermin. They were also used to herd and protect livestock, as well as to hunt badgers and otters.

GENERAL APPEARANCE
The Soft-Coated Wheaten Terrier is a medium-sized dog, measuring an average of 46cm at the shoulder and weighing around 20kg. The most recognisable feature of the breed is its soft, wheaten-coloured coat. The coat should fall naturally in light waves of large loose curls. The Wheaten does not shed, and its single coat should be soft and silky. Wheaten pups are born with dark coats of red, brown, mahogany or white, and usually go through several stages of development before reaching the colour of the adult coat. As the puppy grows, the dark coat grows out to a near white before turning the distinctive wheaten colour that characterises the breed.

PERSONALITY AND TEMPERAMENT
The Soft-Coated Wheaten Terrier is an active and inquisitive dog and, thriving on human interaction, will form a very close bond with its family. This breed is not shy about showing its feelings of affection and loves being the centre of attention. A Wheaten is a good watchdog, and will alert the family to the presence of a stranger. Although watchful, the Wheaten tends not to act aggressively. The Wheaten Terrier does best when involved with the family and less well if left kennelled. As they are very much house dogs, the temperament and personality of this breeds excels in a good home environment.
This breed is the perfect family dog, and gets on well with children and other dogs if socialised early. Being a true terrier, they are more active than other breeds and do require a sufficient amount of exercise to meet these needs. Like the Wheatens of old, today's Wheaten Terriers are adaptable dogs and can live in both city and country environments.

BREED HISTORY

As with many of Ireland's native breeds, very little is known about the origins of the Soft-Coated Wheaten Terrier, although old pictures and records have allowed us to trace them back at least 200 years. Wheatens, bred as an all-purpose farm dog, were an integral part of Irish farming life and aided the farmer in a multitude of daily tasks. Wheatens were used to control vermin, hunt, protect and herd livestock, act as a guard dog, and provide companionship – there is no doubt that Wheatens were the quintessential all-rounder.

Seen as the poor man's dog, Wheatens were shunned by wealthy landowners and gentry who preferred to keep the Irish Wolfhound, a status symbol in Irish society. This was not only a preference, however – it was also law. In 1704, the British enacted a penal code which stated that the Irish Catholic population were not permitted to own dogs worth more than £5. This law lasted for more than a century and had a definite impact on the development of the Wheaten Terrier. The Irish needed a dog that would not draw attention and the moderate local terrier rarely got a second look. This may be the reason it is stressed to this day that the Irish Wheaten Terrier be a moderate dog, with no exaggerated features. Moderation is part of the tradition that kept the Wheaten Terrier a beloved and valued companion to the Irish people for centuries.

CARE

Regular grooming is a must to keep the coat free from mats, and can be particularly intensive from eight to twenty-four months as the puppy coat changes to the adult coat. The Wheaten is an adaptable dog and will thrive in most situations – all that is required is regular exercise and human companionship.

DID YOU KNOW?

Lydia Vogel of Massachusetts is often credited with bringing the first Wheatens to the United States back in the 1940s. In fact, seven Wheaten puppies arrived in Boston on 24 November 1946, and Lydia Vogel came to own two of them. She was the first to show and breed Wheatens in the United States.

Pocadán Ciarraíoch
KERRY BEAGLE
....

FAST, CURIOUS, FRIENDLY

Pocadán Ciarraíoch
KERRY BEAGLE

BREED
Kerry Beagle

LIFESPAN
12–15 years

KENNEL CLUB GROUP
Hound/Not recognised
outside Ireland

VULNERABLE NATIVE BREED
Yes

UTILISATION
The Kerry Beagle is a scent hound, developed primarily for the tracking of stag, but today is used for the tracking of hares, foxes and other small game.

GENERAL APPEARANCE
The Kerry Beagle is a medium-sized hound, standing approximately 61cm tall at the wither and weighing 27kg, with a broad head and long ears. This conformation suggests speed and endurance. This breed has a short, close-lying coat that comes in a variety of colours. Black and tan is the more common colour, although the coat may be tan and white, blue-mottled, tan, solid black or a tricolour of black-tan-white.

PERSONALITY AND TEMPERAMENT
The Kerry Beagle was bred as a specialised pack hound and still exhibits a very strong hunting instinct. In spite of this, they can make an ideal family pet and are friendly, welcoming, and good with children and other dogs. Kerry Beagles are extremely energetic and require a significant amount of exercise on and off leash.

BREED HISTORY
Not your average beagle, it is unclear why the name 'beagle' is attributed to this breed. Actually, the Kerry Beagle is better qualified as a hound. Despite the fact that this breed has never been as small as a beagle, the name has stuck. One possible reason for this connection may lie in the characteristic baying bark of the breed, as the word 'beagle' is thought to derive from the old French word *beegueule*, meaning 'open-mouthed'.

An ancient Irish breed, it is difficult to trace the exact origins of the Kerry Beagle, although many theories have been presented. A possible history of this breed suggests their ancestors were early Celtic hounds, who in later centuries were mixed with other hounds from the Continent to produce the efficient hunting dog we see today. As with all breeds, the Kerry Beagle experienced a rise and fall in popularity, and in the 1800s their numbers suffered a sharp decline due to the Great Famine. During this time, only one major pack was maintained. This particular pack of hounds made up the famous Scarteen pack of county

Limerick, which belonged to the Ryan family. Not only is this pack still in existence, and in the ownership of the Ryan family, it is the pack photographed in this book.

CARE

Energetic and inquisitive, with a strong prey drive, the Kerry Beagle would be best-suited to a home with a generous amount of space, preferably fenced, coupled with owners with an active and outdoor lifestyle. They may not adapt well to apartment living unless their exercise requirements can be fulfilled. Grooming is minimal – occasional brushing and bathing when necessary is all that is required for this dog breed.

DID YOU KNOW?

The Kerry Beagle was taken by many Irish immigrants to the Americas, and is considered a foundation breed in the development of the Coonhound.

Brocaire Uí Mháil

IRISH GLEN OF IMAAL TERRIER

GENTLE, BOLD, SPIRITED

Brocaire Uí Mháil
IRISH GLEN OF IMAAL TERRIER

BREED	LIFESPAN	KENNEL CLUB GROUP	VULNERABLE NATIVE BREED
Irish Glen of Imaal Terrier	12–15 years	Terrier/FCI Group 3	Yes

UTILISATION
The Glen of Imaal Terrier was bred to hunt and eradicate vermin, such as rats, foxes, badgers and otters. A versatile breed, they were also used to herd sheep and cattle on farms, as well as for family companionship. The Glen was bred to work mute and is a silent and deadly hunter. As such, they are known as 'strong dogs', as opposed to 'sounders', who would alert the hunter by barking. The Glen would enter the den of a badger or fox and silently flush out prey, aided by the element of surprise.

GENERAL APPEARANCE
The Glen can be summed up in one phrase: a big dog on short legs. Its size can be deceptive, and although small in stature (only 30–35cm at the shoulder) they can weigh approximately 16kg. This unusual body form allowed the dog to remain close to the ground in order to scent prey and also to fit down narrow dens and sets in search of quarry. Its large body size and weight allowed the voracious dog to tackle large badgers, which in many cases would have been larger than the pursuing dog. Glens have a large head, with half-pricked ears and short, bowed legs. They are unrefined and should never be clipped, as they are a naturally rugged breed. Slow to mature, with three growth phases, a Glen can take three to four years to fully mature. Glens are on average 40% longer than they are tall, and are the only terrier breed not to be defined by a particular colour. The most common colour is wheaten, with variations from red to cream wheaten, blue/silver and brindle, and any combination in between. Wheaten-coloured pups or adolescent dogs often have dark tips to the fur and sometimes a dark strip down the back, but this disappears as the dog matures.

The Glen of Imaal Terrier exhibits an unusual posture, known as 'the Glen sit', not commonly seen in other breeds. This posture sees the dog sitting on its hind legs and holding its entire body in a vertical position.

PERSONALITY AND TEMPERAMENT
Glen of Imaal Terriers are lively and bold. They tend to be more even-tempered than other terrier breeds, more laid-back and far less vocal. A hard-working and explorative dog, they require less attention than other breeds – apart from regular walks, they will happily laze

around the house. They have a stubborn terrier streak and can be independent dogs, but thrive with an owner who is firm and consistent. Unlike some terrier breeds, Glens do well with children and are fiercely loyal to their family, as well as being welcoming and generally calm with strangers. Early socialisation is important, particularly with other dogs and smaller pets within the household, as their prey drive increases with maturity. This breed would be perfect for a busy family, as they love human companionship, but tend not to crave constant attention. Although small, they are strong, plucky dogs; hardy and able to cope and adapt to a variety of situations.

BREED HISTORY

The name of this breed points to its geographical origins in a remote valley, the Glen of Imaal, which is situated in the northern part of the Wicklow Mountains. Under the shadow of the Lugnaquilla mountain, this was an isolated and undisturbed area before the arrival of modern transport.

Looking to Irish lore for some indication as to the origin of the breed is speculative, yet interesting. It is thought that the breed came to the Glen of Imaal during the reign of Elizabeth I, when the French and Hessian soldiers employed to stop rebellion in Ireland brought low-slung hounds with them, who then bred with local terriers to produce the stocky breed we see today.

In the past, dogs did not have the luxury of being pets with no function – they needed to earn their keep and be of use to their owner. They would work around the farm or cottage, keeping vermin under control, hunting, herding and watching the livestock. The breed performed whatever was required of it and thus remained an important part of farm life. Not being popular with the sporting gentry, the breed evolved in this type of setting, untouched by outside influences.

The Glen of Imaal Terrier is also thought to have been used as a turnspit dog. It was commonly agreed that using children as turnspits was inhumane, but the low carriage of the Glen was perfect for turning the wheel of the turnspit, similar to a modern day hamster wheel. The dog would run in the wheel, and by doing so would rotate the spit over the hearth – essentially, a canine-propelled rotisserie. The Glen's highly individualised bowed front legs, well-padded loin and powerful hindquarters were ideally suited to this job.

For several hundred years, these hearty dogs performed their chores in this remote corner of Ireland, unnoticed by all except those who treasured them. Today, the Glen of Imaal Terrier remains one of the rarest breeds of dog in the world.

CARE

Apart from regular walks and early training, this breed is low maintenance. Glens do not shed much and molting is minimal – they require brushing only once a week to keep their coat in good condition and promote healthy skin. A common grooming technique of the breed is hand stripping, a method by which the dead hair is pulled from the coat. Using the proper technique, this is painless for the dog. Historically, the tail was docked, a practice now illegal in Ireland. Docking this breed reduced injury to the tail while hunting and allowed the hunter to pull the dog from a narrow set or den. Overall, Glens are a long-lived, hardy and healthy breed.

DID YOU KNOW?

A story tells of turnspit dogs being taken to church and used as foot warmers. When the bishop gave a sermon and said, 'It was then that Ezekiel saw the *wheel* …' several turnspit dogs ran for the door!

Spáinnéar Uisce

IRISH WATER SPANIEL

....

HARD-WORKING, BRAVE, PLAYFUL

Spáinnéar Uisce
IRISH WATER SPANIEL

BREED	LIFESPAN	KENNEL CLUB GROUP	VULNERABLE NATIVE BREED
Irish Water Spaniel	10–13 years	Gun Dog/FCI Group 8	Yes

UTILISATION
Although the Irish Water Spaniel has been primarily bred to retrieve wildfowl from water, it can be described as a dual-purpose hunting dog, working both water and land. The Water Spaniel will often point and will retrieve readily from heavy cover.

GENERAL APPEARANCE
The Irish Water Spaniel is the largest of the spaniels, ranging in height from 53cm to 59cm at the wither and weighing 25kg to 29kg. A sturdy and cobby dog, the Irish Water Spaniel is ruggedly built, with webbed feet to aid in swimming. Their coat consists of dense curls, which sheds very little. The coat is a unique liver colour, with a definite purple hue. With a naturally smooth face, a topknot of loose curls grows down from the head, often covering the eyes. One of the most distinguishing features of the breed is the smooth rat-like tail, which is completely free of long coat. An overall picture sees the Irish Water Spaniel combining a look of keen intelligence with a strong, solid outline.

PERSONALITY AND TEMPERAMENT
The Irish Water Spaniel thrives in situations where it has a job to do. Bred to hunt and retrieve game with minimal fuss, it has a strong eagerness to please its owners. The breed craves exercise and, as the name suggests, loves water and swimming. Due to its high intelligence level, ability to learn and inquisitive nature, the Irish Water Spaniel has been dubbed 'the clown of the spaniel family' and will find amusing ways to achieve what is asked of it. Early socialisation of the breed is a must, as they can be aloof at first and may be wary of strangers. Generally a quiet dog, they will only bark when they want to warn the family. They make excellent family pets, as they are usually very respectful of children and other pets.

Overall, the Irish Water Spaniel is alert and inquisitive – hard-working and brave in the field, while playful and affectionate at home.

BREED HISTORY

With no real evidence as to the history of the Irish Water Spaniel, tracing its origins is difficult and much of the information available remains obscure and speculative. There is a general understanding that the antecedents of the Irish Water Spaniel originated in Persia and arrived on Irish shores via Spain. It has also been noted that its most distinguishable feature, the rat-like tail, does not appear in any other similar breed, which might suggest that the modern breed, as we know it, is the descendant of an indigenous ancestry. Either way, the breed was highly successful in both hunting and shows, and in 1890 the Irish Water Spaniel Club was formed to promote the interests of the breed.

CARE

A breed with great stamina, these dogs require daily exercise and do best in the suburbs or the countryside. A large outdoor space is ideal, but the breed will happily curl up on the couch once these needs are met. Aside from exercise, the primary consideration for the breed is the maintenance of the coat. The Irish Water Spaniel has a tight double coat, comprising of the longer outer coat and a dense undercoat. The breed sheds very little and may be a more comfortable breed for allergy sufferers. Their coat needs to be brushed through every couple of weeks to promote healthy skin and to remove mats and any burrs or objects that may get caught in the coat. In order to maintain shape, the coat can be cut every few months, which will also reduce the amount of grooming required for a longer coat. Regular exposure to water will help to promote the characteristic curls of the outer coat. The breed is a generally healthy breed.

DID YOU KNOW?

The coat of the Irish Water Spaniel is naturally water-repellent.

Madra Gearr
IRISH TERRIER

· ·

BOLD, DASHING, TENDER-HEARTED

Madra Gearr
IRISH TERRIER

BREED	LIFESPAN	KENNEL CLUB GROUP	VULNERABLE NATIVE BREED
Irish Terrier	13–15 years	Terrier/FCI Group 3	Yes

UTILISATION
Terriers derive their name from the Latin *terra* meaning 'earth'. The breed was originally used to dig into the earth to hunt foxes and otters, as well as to rid the farm of vermin.

GENERAL APPEARANCE
A long-legged terrier, the breed should be longer than it is tall. Standing approximately 45cm at the shoulder and weighing an average of 12kg, this breed is graceful and athletic in appearance and exudes power, speed and strength. Although the breed is tall, it is sturdy and sure-footed and free from clumsiness. It has a lean, muscular frame with a powerful jaw, coupled with a flat skull. The bearded muzzle and bushy eyebrows frame small, dark eyes conveying its alertness and fiery spirit. Their ears are folded into a V-shape, and at times can be darker in colour and shorter in coat than the rest of the body. The outer coat is wiry and dense, and the texture should never be soft, though the breed also has an undercoat, which is softer. The tail was traditionally docked to three-quarters of the original length, a practice since banned in Ireland. The coat is generally a single solid colour, commonly dark red, but also appearing in red, gold or wheaten.

PERSONALITY AND TEMPERAMENT
With all the characteristics of a typical terrier, the Irish Terrier is a courageous daredevil – bold and spirited. Although not a large dog, what they lack in size they make up for with their huge personality. Known to be fearless, the Irish Terrier needs a firm and consistent owner. Early socialisation of the breed is a must, as due to their nature they may be combatant and dominant towards other dogs and small pets, but if trained early this will not be a problem. The breed enjoys training and can as such be trained easily, having an eagerness to please. These traits ensure that they are seen in a variety of competitions, such as agility and obedience.

Despite their bold nature they make brilliant family pets. They are totally devoted to their family and are extremely affectionate, loving human interaction and attention. They make very good guard dogs and are extremely protective of their family, home and territory. While active, they are not hyperactive, and are relaxed at home.

BREED HISTORY

One of the oldest breeds of terrier, the exact origins of the Irish Terrier are unknown. It is thought that its origins may be linked to the rough-coated black and tan terrier bred by the ancient Britons. In fact, in earlier generations of the breed it was quite common for bitches to whelp black and tan pups in their litters, which some speculate may be caused by this black and tan terrier heritage. Even today in the modern Irish Terrier, pups may be born with black shading, which disappears as the pup matures.

Originally, the Irish Terrier was bred for function rather than looks. This approach led to a wide variety within the breed, in both size and colour. For years the Irish Terrier came in a variety of colours: black and tan, grey and brindle, wheaten of all shades, and, of course, red. The size of an individual dog also varied, which is evident by the fact that at the Exhibition Palace Show held in Dublin in 1874 there were individual classes for Irish Terriers over 9lb and under 9lb. Clearly, size or colour did not matter, provided the dog could perform the function for which it was intended.

As the breed evolved, Irish Terriers became popular in the show ring, and thus pedigrees were kept. However, the differences in some strains of the breed presented confusion for judges and breeders alike as to the breed standard of the true Irish Terrier. So, in 1879 the first Irish Terrier Club was formed in Dublin and a breed standard was drawn up, and this is the standard that all modern Irish Terriers are modelled on. In this same momentous year, the champion bitch, Erin, made her first appearance, along with Killiney Boy. It was with the union of these two dogs, known as the mother and father of the breed, that the Irish Terrier's future was cemented. Today it would be difficult to find a modern pedigree that does not go back to these two Irish Terriers.

During the World War I, the Irish Terrier showed its usefulness, when, due to their extraordinary intelligence and fearlessness, they were trained as guard dogs and messengers for soldiers. On the battlefield the dogs were referred to as 'Micks' or 'Paddys', and it was said that the Irish Terrier could work longer and harder on a bowl of biscuits than 'any other living creature'. The Irish Terrier today endures as the fearless devil of yesteryear, and their intelligence and courage remain very much intact.

CARE

An extremely versatile breed, the Irish Terrier is adaptable to apartment or city living and is brilliant with children. The wiry coat of a pet Irish Terrier needs minimal grooming, and stripping the coat once or twice a year will keep its water-resistant qualities. Irish Terriers, if shown, will require specialist grooming on a regular basis.

DID YOU KNOW?

The Irish Terrier has the distinction of being the only all-red terrier.

Brocaire Gorm

KERRY BLUE TERRIER

SMART, ALERT, PEOPLE-ORIENTED

Brocaire Gorm
KERRY BLUE TERRIER

BREED	LIFESPAN	KENNEL CLUB GROUP	VULNERABLE NATIVE BREED
Kerry Blue Terrier	12–15 years	Terrier/FCI Group 3	Yes

UTILISATION

The Kerry Blue Terrier was originally bred to control vermin. Aside from this, the breed also served as a general working dog on many Irish farms and managed a variety of jobs, such as protecting livestock and guarding property. Like all native terriers, the Kerry Blue excelled on Irish farms as an adaptable, multi-functional working breed.

Seeing a Kerry Blue in full show trim is a spectacular sight, and the coat is a key feature of the breed. Their coat comes in several shades of blue, but pups are born black, turning progressively blue/grey as they mature. The coat is soft, wavy and dense, with a texture comparable to human hair. Kerry Blues are non-shedding, and their coat will continue to grow if left untrimmed. Because of this, they are often recommended for people with allergies or asthma, although it is advisable to spend time with the breed first to check whether or not they are suitable for you.

GENERAL APPEARANCE

The Kerry Blue Terrier is a muscular, medium-sized breed, standing 45–49cm at the shoulder, and weighing 15–18kg. They have long heads and small V-shaped ears, with a long neck that widens towards the shoulders. The tail is medium length, set high and straight.

PERSONALITY AND TEMPERAMENT

Kerry Blue Terriers are fun-loving and intensely loyal companions. They are extremely affectionate and playful at heart, and they thrive in a home environment. While loving to members of the family, the Kerry Blue can be headstrong, feisty and boisterous. Early socialisation of this breed is an absolute must, and should be kept up throughout their adult life. Due to their strong prey drive and typical terrier characteristics, they can be dominant and combative towards other dogs. Exposure to other dogs and strangers from a young age will produce a well-rounded adult dog and a perfect companion and family pet, though they may do better with older children. Kerry Blues do best with an authoritative owner who has a knowledge of dog behaviour and who can offer firm, consistent training. They can be highly protective of their family and this should not be overly encouraged. Generally a quiet breed, they rarely bark unnecessarily. Although a self-assured breed, these dogs excel when trained and, being highly intelligent and intuitive, do best when given a job to do.

BREED HISTORY

Delving into the origins of the Kerry Blue Terrier is both a frustrating and fascinating experience – during the time the breed emerged there were no records kept, and thus no one knows with certainty when the breed emerged. In light of this, one might be inclined to reprimand the Irish people for not keeping a better record of their breeding stock. However, the Irish were one of the first to record pedigrees and undertake a systematic and organised approach to dog breeding in general. In fact, ancient Brehon Law outlined laws pertaining to dog breeding, welfare and ownership.

Although definitive information is lacking, it is certainly interesting to look toward Irish mythology and folklore for an interesting insight into the possible origins of this breed – how much is true and how much is pure fiction, however, it is near impossible to say. It is true that in the past the nobility in Ireland were the only people permitted to own (and hunt with) Irish Wolfhounds, and it has been speculated that the peasantry developed the Kerry Blue Terrier for the purpose of poaching, in response to this ban. There is a legend of a magnificent 'Blue Dog' that made its way to shore from a ship wrecked off the coast of Kerry, often cited as being of the Spanish Armada. This dog proceeded to mate with local terriers, and its offspring started the Kerry Blue Terrier breed.

The Portuguese Water Dog has also been linked with the origins of the breed, partly due to the similarity of coat, but also due to the regular trading and bartering of animals between Ireland and the British Isles, and subsequently, Spain and Portugal. These viewpoints are all up for discussion and there can be no doubt that further research on the origins of the Kerry Blue is needed.

The Kerry Blue was first shown in Ireland in 1916. Initially shown untrimmed and with its natural rugged look, once the breed gained recognition in England and entered the British show ring it was trimmed and tidied up, giving rise to the Kerry Blue Terrier we see today.

CARE

Due to the non-shedding nature of the Kerry Blue Terrier's coat, the breed requires a trim every six weeks and a full brush through once a week. The beard may need cleaning more often to keep it clean and free of debris and food. Kerry Blues need to be exercised regularly, and early training and socialisation of the breed is a necessity. They can live in apartments or the countryside, provided they are given enough stimulation to keep their active and intelligent minds occupied.

DID YOU KNOW?

Irish revolutionary leader Michael Collins was both an owner and exhibitor of the Kerry Blue Terrier. Collins' best-known Kerry Blue was named 'Convict 224'. Collins even attempted to elevate the Kerry Blue to the status of the National Dog of Ireland. However, there are no known records of this legislation having been passed.

Sotar Rua agus Bán

IRISH RED & WHITE SETTER

COURAGEOUS, SPIRITED, DETERMINED

Sotar Rua agus Bán
IRISH RED & WHITE SETTER

BREED	LIFESPAN	KENNEL CLUB GROUP	VULNERABLE NATIVE BREED
Irish Red & White Setter	10–12 years	Gun Dog/FCI Group 7	Yes

UTILISATION

The function of setters is to locate game, such as grouse, partridge, pheasant and snipe. Carrying its head high, trying to locate the scent of game in the air, the dog quarters the ground methodically and systematically. Once the game is located the dog adopts the characteristic 'set', by freezing on point in a lowered crouching position; its frame will be rigid and tense as it focuses on the hidden birds. This setting stance points the handler to exactly where the game is located. In short, the Irish Red and White Setter allows the hunter to find and pinpoint the exact location of birds. In the past, the birds would have been caught using a net, but the use of the modern automatic rifle has replaced this practice.

GENERAL APPEARANCE

The main distinguishing feature of the Irish Red and White Setter is its colour. As the name suggests, Irish Red and White Setters should be red and white. One of the best descriptions of the breed is given by Lord Rossmore in 1944:

> The colour of the red and white setter is most important. White should predominate and form the background or major colour. The red should only appear in large blotches. The boundary between red and white should be clearly defined. Although the boundary may be irregular, there should be no gradual blending of colour between red and white. The head should carry a red blotch, but the muzzle should be white. The ears should be red. There should be no specks on the body, but freckles on the nose and feet are allowed. The tail may be all white, but if marked with a red blotch is improved. They were easily trained, and to a keen sportsman quite the most pleasurable and keen dogs to shoot over and have as a friend that any man could wish.
>
> (*Irish Dogs*, W. L. Cuddy, 1978)

The coat is short and flat around the head and body. Feathering can be seen on the outer edges of the ears, neck, chest, down the back of the front legs, under the belly and on the back legs. The tail is also feathered, with its coat particularly long here. The feathering should not be too exaggerated, and never curly. No specific weight is given in the kennel club breed standard, but males can be up to 66cm at the shoulder and weigh around 32kg.

PERSONALITY AND TEMPERAMENT

The Irish Red and White Setter is a loyal and attentive companion and makes for the perfect family dog. Generally submissive and non-assertive, they are a gentle and welcoming breed. Essentially a working dog, they do best in active households where they can expel some of their energy, and do require enough space to run freely so they can gallop and act on their natural searching instincts. Although energetic outdoors, they are quiet and calm indoors, preferring to curl up on the couch. Extremely sweet-natured, they are exceptional with children and other dogs.

BREED HISTORY

'Setting dogges' have been used for centuries. By the 17th century these 'setting dogges' were well-established, although during this period interbreeding of different colours was still taking place. Gradually, breeders started to selectively breed dogs depending on their suitability to the working terrain.

Originally in Ireland, setting dogs came in a variety of colours, with most being red, particolour red and white, or nearly all white. These colours were interbred readily, and so all setting dogs in Ireland, regardless of colour, were classed under the umbrella term 'Irish Setter'. In the mid-19th century there were mixed views on the exact colour of the Irish Setter, and by the end of the century there was a notable move towards a solid red colour. During this time the red and white coloured dogs suffered a sharp decline in popularity and numbers reached such low numbers that many thought the breed extinct. It was only with the great efforts of Irishman, Rev. Noble Huston, that the breed survived extinction. In 1970, there was a revival of the breed, and today the Irish Red and White Setter can be found across the world. Comparative to other breeds, however, numbers are still low, and so it is classed as a vulnerable breed.

CARE

Irish Red and White Setters must be provided with a decent amount of exercise and the space to run free, as well as a weekly brush, but other than that the breed is low maintenance. Overall, they are a healthy breed.

DID YOU KNOW?

The Irish Red and White Setter, along with the Irish Red Setter, appeared on an Irish postage stamp during the early 1900s.

Sotar Rua

IRISH RED SETTER

GRACEFUL, SWEET-NATURED, ACTIVE

Sotar Rua
IRISH RED SETTER

BREED	LIFESPAN	KENNEL CLUB GROUP	VULNERABLE NATIVE BREED
Irish Red Setter	10–12 years	Gun Dog/FCI Group 7	No

UTILISATION

The Irish Red Setter is a gun dog, and searches for game silently and methodically. When the dog comes across prey it freezes, rather than giving chase. The setter gets its name from the distinctive crouch or 'set' it adopts when it encounters prey, which indicates to the hunter where the quarry is located. Once the prey is located the birds are then flushed out from the cover, allowing the hunters to get a clear shot. While trying to locate a scent, Irish Red Setters will systematically cover the ground with their head held high as they try to pick up the airborne scent of game birds. The Red Setter should never follow a foot scent.

GENERAL APPEARANCE

There can be no doubt that the Irish Red Setter is one of the most beautiful and graceful of all breeds. Athletic in conformation, this dog stands over two foot tall at the shoulder, ranging from 58cm to 67cm and weighing from 27kg to 32kg. The breed is slightly longer than it is tall. Their most notable feature is their medium length, silky coat, which comes in a rich deep red or chestnut colour. During colder winter months the coat develops a dense undercoat. Their coat is feathered longer in certain places – a feature that can be seen on the tail, chest, ears, legs and underside of the body. This gives the dog an elegant, flowing appearance.

PERSONALITY AND TEMPERAMENT

Irish Red Setters are an active and intelligent breed, and require long daily walks and exercise. Once these demands are met, they make the perfect family pet. Naturally submissive, they do well in a family setting and are very good with children. Eager to please, they thrive on human companionship and make excellent companion dogs. Due to the hunting nature of this breed it is best if they have an enclosed exercise area. Training from an early age is essential as they have a tendency to 'play deaf' when off leash, so recall training is very important. This dog will thrive in an active household, particularly when given a job to do. If left alone for long periods, they may become hyperactive and destructive in an attempt to alleviate energy. Overall, the Irish Red Setter is a loving and affectionate dog.

BREED HISTORY

As is evident throughout this book, the tracing of breed history is a difficult task. One of the earliest references to a 'setting' type dog can be found within the literature of John Caius in his work *De Canibus Britannicis* (*Of English Dogges*), first published in 1576. Although the original is written in Latin, the translated passage reads:

> The Dogge called the Setter, in Latine *Index*.
> Another sort of Dogges be there, serviceable for fowling, making no noise either with foote or with tongue, whiles they followe the game. These attend diligently upon theyr master and frame their conditions to such beckes, motions, and gestures, as it shall please him to exhibite and make, either going forward, drawing backeward, inclining to the right hand, or yealding toward the left, (In making mencion of fowles, my meaning is of the Partridge & the Quaile) when he hath founde the byrde, he keepeth sure and fast silence, he stayeth his steppes and will proceede no further, and with a close, covert, watching eye, layeth his belly to the grounde and so creepeth forward like a worme. When he approacheth neere to the place where the byrde is, he layes him downe, and with a marcke of his pawes betrayeth the place of the byrdes last abode, whereby it is supposed that this kinde of dogge is called *Index*, Setter, being in deede a name most consonant and agreeable to his quality.

It would be unwise to assume that the above-mentioned dog and the Irish Red Setter we know today are the same, or even resembled one another at all, but it is clear that the same behaviours can still be witnessed in the modern setter. The dog Caius mentions is long since extinct, but we can presume it to be an early foundation breed that eventually gave rise to the setters we find today, the Irish Red Setter among them.

It is generally accepted that the Irish Red and White Setter gave rise to the Irish Red Setter, but the two breeds have co-existed alongside one another for over two centuries. Indeed, it was in the 1800s that a preference for a solid-colour setter started to take effect within the breed. With selective breeding within showing circles, a dog of solid red was produced, giving rise to the breed we now call the Irish Red Setter. Before this, the Irish Setter could be seen in a myriad of colours. There is a notable difference in show ring Red Setters and working Red Setters: the working dogs tend to be lighter in weight, around 20kg, and in colour, sometimes showing a russet, and even fawn, colour.

Today there is a concerted effort to bring back the field abilities of the show dogs, to such an extent that many dogs can be seen in both the ring and the field. The breed standard for the modern Irish Setter was first drawn up by the Irish Red Setter Club in Dublin and approved on 29 March 1886.

CARE

With a silky medium-length coat, regular grooming is required to keep it free of mats. Overall, a healthy breed, once exercised and given attention the breed needs little else to keep it happy.

DID YOU KNOW?

Contrary to popular belief, the three setters – English, Gordon and Irish – are not merely different colours or varieties that fall under one 'setter' heading, but are in fact three separate breeds.

BE A RESPONSIBLE DOG OWNER

Dogs as companions are simply unmatched in their loyalty, devotion and affection. Anyone who has ever had the opportunity to love a dog will attest to the unconditional love and happiness they bring to our lives. Owning a dog is an amazing experience, but more than that it is a huge responsibility.

Dogs rely on their owners for everything, from food to shelter, but deserve so much more than just the basics. Bringing a dog into your life is a big commitment, and the onus is on you to educate yourself to the seriousness and longevity of such an undertaking. If you are interested in obtaining a native Irish dog breed please contact the Irish Kennel Club, who will be able to help and advise you.

ACKNOWLEDGEMENTS

This book would not have been possible without the help of a few generous people. Firstly, thank you to the breeders (listed below) who allowed us to photograph their beautiful dogs and who gave up many hours of their precious time. Thank you to the Irish Kennel Club, particularly Sean Delmar, who provided guidance throughout the project and expertise at every turn.

To the publishing team at Currach Press who worked so hard on producing the beautiful book you hold in your hands, thank you all. Lastly, to the fabulous dogs photographed, always a wagging tail and a warm welcome, hail, rain or shine – thank you.

Irish Wolfhound: Tony Dunne, Gerry Clarke
Irish Soft-Coated Wheaten Terrier: Elaine Butler, Jennifer Kealy, Fergus O'Sullivan, Bernadette Moynihan, Lesley Porter, Ruth Nesbitt, Susan Kealy
Kerry Beagle: Chris Ryan
Irish Glen of Imaal Terrier: Nicky White, Anne White
Irish Water Spaniel: Emma O'Donnell, Mark O'Donnell, Shauna O'Donnell, Amanda Kilkenny
Irish Terrier: John Canty, Moss Dowling, Mick Doyle, Frank Byrne, Laura Carroll
Kerry Blue Terrier: Harold Quigg, Helena Quigg, Darwin Martin, Paul Burke, Michael Marley, Gerry Daly, Fionnuala Malone
Irish Red & White Setter: Vince Flannery, Nessa O'Donoghue
Irish Red Setter: Aidan Dunne, Trudy Walsh, Kay Donnelly, Chris Kane

We have endeavoured to include all who helped with the book on this list. If we have inadvertently omitted anyone, we offer our sincere apologies, and will be happy to correct this on any future editions.

First published in 2015 by Currach Press
23 Merrion Square North
Dublin 2
Co. Dublin
Ireland
www.currach.ie

ISBN: 978-1-78218-892-6

Set in Averta 9/12
Book design by Helene Pertl | Currach Press
Printed by Jellyfish Solutions